The Kindness of the Eel

Ben Ray

smith|doorstop

Published 2020 by Smith|Doorstop Books
The Poetry Business
Campo House,
54 Campo Lane,
Sheffield S1 2EG
www.poetrybusiness.co.uk

ISBN 978-1-912196-28-9
Designed & Typeset by Utter
Printed by Biddles

Smith|Doorstop books are a member of Inpress:
www.inpressbooks.co.uk. Distributed by NBN International, 1 Deltic Avenue,
Rooksley, Milton Keynes, MK13 8LD.

The Poetry Business gratefully acknowledges the support of
Arts Council England.

Contents

"I think you can't really reflect life's broad scope without the documentation, without the human evidence. The picture will not be complete."
– Svetlana Alexievich

The Thoughts of Charles Byrne

*The skeleton of 'the Irish giant' Charles Byrne (1761-1783) is
displayed, against his will, at the Hunterian Museum, London.*

when the sun went down and darkness crept in, slick as an afterthought
and I fell off the tongue of God like the last line of the sacrament
I said to George, I told him, don't let them take me, my earthly carriage
is my own – bury me within the water, I beg you, don't let them touch
(We gath. arnd his deathbd quickly, nay, I am nt ashmd to say, eagrly)
Dr. Mawton of Chelsea

Lord, I know I was mean once: as a child I killed a dog that came close
dropped the stone from my height like a judgement, and then – yes
the nails digging into palms, bent double to allow Pa's beating
*(The subject is 7ft. 7in. tall, this remarkable condition brought on
by some abnormality – evidence of pituitary tumour at base of skull)*
medical report, 1909

was it this, George, tell me what is the reason I have stood to attention
for all this taut time, wires binding my chafing limbs – was it the drink
surely it cannot be His Will that my crown's closeness to the heavens
keeps me from the sleeping earth He calls the remaining world to
*(His grand Height originating, it is heard from certain Reliable Quarters
from his being conceived on the Top of an exceedingly tall Haystack)*
The Herald Newspaper, 1782

why do I remember the dirt between the seat-crammed rows
the applause as I danced for unknown eager faces behind lights
crowds as I lit my pipe off the lamp lights on Cowgate Bridge, all those
catcalls and handclaps which gave relieved thanks they were not me
where was that place, George, tell me – sometimes I forget, where am I
*(We saw him drink from a teapot, it was right frightful to watch
Mama told me he would eat us if we did not go to bed when told)*
Sarah Price, audience member

I once knew Elspeth at the Royal, arms broad from too many days' work
a chest that beckoned you in, eyes that could swallow a week's savings

I'll have another round, Elspeth, and one for yourself
(And 1 shilling for the driver, and 10 shillings for the law
to avert its omniscient gaze and to get the object away to safety)

John Hunter, surgeon

I was stripped – a shocking act, my self stolen and boiled from my bones
where am I, George, I am not home, I can tell; no, not gone yet
(The specimen is a wonder to behold, with a normal man placed beside
in order to accentuate the medical event for all of us to see)

Richard Gables, medical student

oh, I have been held still for longer than I breathed this very air
I am tired, George, so tired, just let me kneel

lie down on the seabed's blessed floor

Meditation on Three 15th Century Wooden Barrels Found Within a Shipwreck in Gdansk harbour

To him they carry the vain dream of another morning
but in truth they contain copper ingot, meant for coins
to rival the silver cobs belched into Europe
from the unimaginable Potosí. These objects
have travelled further than he ever will, Lübeck to Oslo
to Madrid to London in a cobweb of pathways
sketched by minds a thousand miles away onto the ocean
that pumps life into the markets of the world
and that pushes the present into the future.
It does not occur to him if this is all worth dying for: instead
his coldness ebbs away and he has, all of a sudden
a sense of melancholy –
of the sort that one sometimes feels
when grey light falls on grey surfaces

Family Photo Album: Tunisia, 1996

for the Hemons

In nearly every shot, your green dress ruffles softly in unseen wind
like a cry. It is late June, air hot as coffee and cheeks red as peppers
as you shed your old skins amongst the umbrellas and ice creams.
'Don't worry, Mačka Hvala,' your mother always said
'lucky children don't burn,' and so you'd escape into the breakers
under a borderless sky with the universal gasp of skin on seawater.
They're crumbling now, the plastic slips you keep yourselves in
the brittleness of memories eating away at their edges,
a meticulous reality of restauranted evenings and of photo timers
here you are on the log flume – your fringe was longer then
(all girls had their hair this way, it was the Sarajevo style)
here's you playing confused decoy, told to sit still
as your mother surreptitiously snaps the first black man
either of you had seen. In this one, your mother grasps your hand
but she is looking away, above the camera, perhaps
to a future you will now never have, where Party badges glint in the sun
where 'T' stands not for *tata* but for Tito. Or perhaps
to the afternoon when two hundred Muslims were thrown from cliffs
and she managed to rescue three boys from the wreckage.
There is no photo of this. Instead, there is just you two, here:
her handhold is tight, the knuckles white and strained
trying to keep you in this moment: trying to keep you from
that fishbowl shaken city where the walls are all halved
and people do not dare to cross the street

The Bird Wound Man is in a Bedsit in Inverness

The Bird Wound Man, or Feur Eun Lota in Gaelic, was originally a Scottish pre-Christian ritual where birds were encouraged by an individual to attack the body, with the resulting scars being interpreted as heavenly text in a conversation between the human, the avian and the angelic.

and is opening his arms slowly like harbour doors
palms facing upward in invitation, in asking

south by south east, to warmer air where bugs sit waiting on hard earth

eager to surrender his human bearings in search
of voices he thinks he does not know already

trees two days northward: warmth, sleep, then call for others and flock

Feur Eun Lota: cicatrix as language, his flesh
a drawing board where avian and angelic collide

dark shadow in the above, fear fear quick speed back to nest

he is hungry, he aches for the pieces he is convinced
are missing: what more, he asks, I must know, there must be

rest now, move when heat is high in midday: much food west, over water

The Knee Plays: Act I

Knee plays were short, disconnected scenes interspersed throughout theatrical performances in the Tudor period. These scenes would occur in front of the drop curtain and wouldn't require large sets or crowds, thus allowing time for larger costume and scene changes. They had no relation to the overall plot of the play but instead worked as 'joints' allowing the scenes to flex and work together, thus earning them their unique name.

Sc. 1. At night I wonder if the border guard stole your passport

and changed places with you:
is he out there somewhere, living an alternate life
drinking that tea with orange you like
wearing the jewellery you got from your mother.
In bed, your hands feel perfunctory
searching me methodically, looking for something
they cannot find

Sc. 2. The day before we leave forever, we take a photo

Out of house in ones careful careful now / Shanghai is quiet and so are we / no leave the lights on so no one knows / for the Red Guard are my classmates who swapped football for cruelty / and their objectives are sharp as knives / in darkness the street is a river that we cross / by feeling the stones underwater / now window, room, secret wink of a tripod / that will tell us to each other / if we separate along the way / mother: dress now too large, nails bitten / father: eyes already elsewhere, body twitching / me: squinting, fascinated by the light / one each, one each, mother tells the man / in case we have to find each other / when we left next day, crouched in a lorry bed / I was thinking of the fourth face my photo did not contain / his tired fingers pressing the shutter / I wonder what happened to him

Sc. 3. Switzerland has announced plans to abolish the emergency stockpiling of coffee

Headline from the Guardian, 10th April 2019

In what became known as The Mistake
the Swiss stopped the emergency stockpiling of coffee
how could humanity have known the Virus' only cure
was a half-brewed macchiato with milk at 3°C and cocoa sprinkles?
We are the stragglers, but we cannot hide here for long
soon the Italians will find us

Metamorphoses

'Those buggers are just amazing.'
The fisherman catches your sleeve,
ancient mariner of the marina
rod angled hopefully into the water.
'Did you know, contrary to popular opinion
salmon move in careful formation in open waters?'
I bestow a rictus grin. Tighten our handhold.
'And they return to the spot they hatched from to spawn.
Do you know where their name comes from?'
I step back, but you wriggle from my grip.
'From the Latin "salmo", you say,
'which may have come from "salire", meaning "to leap".'
I give you a surprised look, but you are away
locked in a slow, hypnotic dance.
'Salmon hatch in fresh water, but migrate to the sea,'
he leans in, and you respond in echo
'but they return to fresh water to reproduce.'
And as you move in synchronicity, circling, twisting
I can only watch as you interpret each other
an intimate game, up on tiptoes, turning
until finally he slides off the harbour edge into the sea
        and I know I should say something
                but before I manage to, you follow
      and I can only think to watch
                  as you both move away
        bodies flicking, as if in formation

The Schéchenyi Thermal Baths, Budapest: a love poem

This pool contains calcium magnesium sodium
when it's whirled we can smell the otherness of it
it's no wonder that we   come out different people

That stag party in from Prague   talking Pilsner & Budweiser have
arrived, laid claim to this space   so we go, sink into another pool.
Underwater our bodies lift, echo   each other.   There is something
slowing   about the water here   something still. Hold me tighter

We move
from cold to hot to cold again
sweat glistening on our arms and on our legs
our nakedness belying the volumes we carry with us
from pool to pool. You say something, but
it is lost, like this metaphor
in the steam

You told me once you trusted water,   that you loved the inevitability of
its movements. Now, held in two embraces, you only talk of how white
the tiled bottom is; how the light from the roof stretches miles to reach
it; how the water's edge seems suddenly so far off, the earth so distant

These baths were built in
1913 by men who swam in luxury and
who did not see the deluge ahead of them. It is easy
to understand this, when the water is always washing tomorrow
away. I find that I don't care about tomorrow either
come with me to the next pool, darling
the water is warmer there

The Discovery

Today they found the ship
Herodotus had described
over two thousand years ago
lying still like a secret
under dark waters
silently shoring up his words
with its hard timber ribs
mooring itself at last
alongside our consciousness.
Will I too be found
in some unthinkable future
will the measurement tape
circle my temples, and confirm
that I existed, that I loved
and was loved, that I gave
and was given to – or will I appear
under clumsy, careless fingers
that have no knowledge
of who they touch

The Last Druidic Bard in Wales

The Last Druidic Bard in Wales lives in a caravan outside Cardiff
and writes odes whilst on the piss. There's mould above his bed
and the neighbours have complained about the noise.
(He says it's artistic expression; they say it's Dolly Parton at 3am.)

As he's The Last Druidic Bard in Wales, the government quickly declares
his poems National Treasures, debuted in the Cardiff Millennium Centre
usually accompanied by interpretive dance from an enthusiastic group
from Cwmystwyth's University of the Third Age (no one's sure why).

The Last Druidic Bard in Wales is invited annually to the Eisteddfod
where he spends all his complementary festival tickets on Old Scrumpy
and cracks lewd jokes in his BBC Wales interview with Huw Edwards,
each year his anecdotes about Owain Glyndŵr changing ever so slightly.

The Last Druidic Bard in Wales is on the night-bus out of Newport
swearing at the bus driver for not using the tongue of his grandmother
and because he is The Last Druidic Bard in Wales no one says anything
even though the driver moved down here from Leeds in '92.

And when The Last Druidic Bard in Wales misses another deadline
for the opening of a youth centre because the rugby's on
or tells the reading group not to go to Anglesey, there's no decent pubs
or when he coughs a little too hard and is left doubled over

people wince and avert their eyes, unwilling to imagine a world that only
conformed

The Knee Plays: Act II

Sc. 1. Breakfast

It has snowed again
and, of course, we have eaten it
gobbling it up impatiently
dragging tongues along the gutters
always concerned this may be
our last meal before spring

Sc. 2. Herons

That day we saw two herons
playing chess in the sky above us
so careful, so considered
we were returning from your uncle's
where you'd balanced plum stones
on my plate, and had berated me
for damaging the spiders' webs.
This poem wasn't meant to be about you
but sometimes herons land in the strangest places.

Sc. 3. Inheritance

Father, you've given me this globe | this burnt heirloom round my neck,
Mother, I'm thankful for your path | I'll spend my life gathering its parts
and I know that | when my time comes

I will do the same

The Kindness of the Eel

You opened your mouth
and an eel came out –
sliding from between your lips
gasping into the air.

Take this, you said
these are my best words
my midnight flights
my early morning distillations.

Eels, you said, do not stutter
look, they flow like liquid
they do not take more than they need
they are the best of us.

I watched it swim away
out of the bedroom window.
But often, when I least expect it
it returns, a slow swagger through the air:

brushing past the curtains when I sleep
curling into the nest of my inner ear.

What I Heard on the World's Last Cassette Player

When I dug out the spools of tape
they were lying in a reptilian nest of noises
twisted in nakedness, locked in hibernation.
I fished them out, softly, oh so slowly
but still they woke up, disturbed: I watched
as they spooled around my fingers like creeping things.
In the unflattering truth of kitchen bulbs they hissed
and flicked, bending the light, eager to wriggle back home
but I caught them before they escaped
wound their flexing forms around a pencil
and took them to the Last Cassette Player in the World.
It was lying, slumped in its cage – a bird on a sphere
that had no sky to spare, mouth open for a dead language.
Its curator and I fed the worms between the analogue lips,
finding dust-coated buttons with a firm touch.
And softly, oh so slowly, it began to sing.

It sang	of Maoris	of engines thrumming
cockle-pickers	out on empty sands	I don't understand
what are fish	in the colour-seeped	deep sandpaper rust
hear this	men in shallow graves	buildings so tall
the sky is pierced	the sun is too bright	what so many gone
we did not think	fingers on skin clawing	holding knowing listen
hhsss	hhsss	hhsss click

The curator and I exchanged glances.
He nodded, and I collected up the strands of tape
that fell dead at our feet. They did not move.
Then I took them to the garden,
where I laid them in the cold earth so slowly,
so softly, oh so slowly

Interview with Female Members of the Solidarność Movement

Featuring: Mrs. Bartkowicz (A), Mrs. Mazur (B), Mrs. Nowak (C), Mrs. Wójcik (D), Mrs. Kozłowski (E)

I remember driving out of Warsaw in '89, right after the free elections ᴬ

that sense of space. Under communism, see, there was no emancipation: men and women, we were all oppressed, in it together ᴮ

and they relied on us, the men. Those strong arms, those confident hands grasping banners, those voices you can hear from your radio – we were their support, their lungs ᴰ

with rolodexes in our heads! ᴱ

With transistor radios and samizdat in our prams! Where the authorities never thought to look ᶜ

under martial law they took all the men, left us as halves. A farmyard with no cockerels, just imagine! But not empty ᴮ

no, not alone! ᴱ

We created networks of safe-houses, a country-wide web led by our Arachnes – publishing ᶜ

Tygodnik Solidarność, yes! The voice of Solidarity! And we launched women on the airwaves, remember? ᴰ

I remember. We told all the listeners to switch their lights on, then went to the roof and all of Warsaw was alight as if on fire again ᴮ

I cried. ᶜ

We were the implementers. What do you do with sudden power? The world was upside down, and we were ᴰ

everything! For a time. And everybody knew, and nobody said. Us, the invisible ones ᴮ that even the men didn't see when they returned. And then Wałesa was back and that was [E]

that. You can escape the regime, but not normality [D]

we fell back to being the natural second. We were their lungs, but never their voice [C]

no, never the voice. Of course not, it had never been that way. [B]

A friend, she said to me: Who will remember us to our own country? [C]

That first escape after it all, leaving the city – do you remember driving out of Warsaw in '89, after the free elections? [A]

Of course. The road ran from my feet to Paris. I'd never felt so free [E]

it was built from concrete blocks, I remember: one after another after another, each bump in the road a small step leading to a better place [A]

Morning After

Rome seems oppressively sad ... the abundance of fragments of the past (on which a tiny present nourishes itself) that have been fetched out of the ground and laboriously maintained ... are basically nothing more than accidental vestiges of another age and a life that is not our own and is not meant to be.
– from *Letters to a Young Poet* (Rainer Maria Rilke)

But look, how the ageless city has aged
plaster cracking on sunken cheeks.
Your foundation does not blend
with your complexion, my darling
the smile that won't quite cover broken teeth
unable to hide the fingernails that dropped off
your delicate digits of Corinthian and Doric.
And if all roads still lead to you, my dear
is this the welcome that you will give them?
Time the great undresser long ago
got wise to your amphitheatrics
and confiscated your frescoed chic –
left with residual mosaic rashes, old tattoos
I fear surgery cannot save your cranial gaps

> now tell me, please, how is it
> that the bones of this place
> this city of light we built together
> the bones of this place, look, tell me please
> quick are they showing beneath the silk
> these veins under each other's skin, this paper-feel
> lethargy it seeps into limbs that touch and twine
> under winding, all too transparent sheets

The Somnambulists

In April 2019 the roof of the 12th century cathedral Notre-Dame de Paris burnt down – however, it was learnt later that the beehives kept on the building's roof had survived the fire.

Last night I dreamt I was wandering in a hollow space
calling out for bees. I know that you were too
that we just failed to find each other there.
And then, today, they announced in the papers
that those hives all nestled close like kisses
in between the wooden ribs had somehow survived.
A modern miracle, they said – the queen lives.

When I woke this morning it was all over the radio
the hives of Our Lady had been saved. But somehow
their memory holds such clarity: the cavity in my head
where their buzz used to be, it was clearer
than the shaky camera phone footage you see
of soldiers reunited with their daughters
of plane crashes where everyone survives
all the good things they tell us are happening

I had a dream last night I dreamt I was calling out
for them. The bees I mean well anyway
and then on the television now
those hives alive swarming. I wonder
if it's true. Last night in bed held between states
I felt myself call out and for a moment my voice
joined a thousand thousand others calling
stretching out through the Anthropocene
all calling for the bees to come back

The Knee Plays: Act III

Sc. 1. Scipio and Aemilia whisper to each other in the darkness

And after she has done it, she rises up his body
like the spring tide, to lie on his panting chest.
Silence presses in on their naked skin.
'What shall I do for you?' His lips brush her ear.
'Destroy Carthage,' she whispers.

Sc. 2. The nationalist pauses on the barricades

Why does national determinism always lead
to statehood, the nationalist wondered.
Why can we not just self-terminate
in a glorious puff of paperwork
and instead of shouting and waving flags
spend the afternoon on the beach –
a nation determined to determine
an independent state of mind

Sc. 3. Land reform: a radicalist's manifesto

1. Move all climate deniers to the coast
2. Give the grouse control of Scotland
3. Drown Liverpool to give Machynlleth fresh water
4. Northern Ireland: oh I don't know, just toss a coin
5. Return all Manx cats to the Isle of Man
6. Relocate London to the North, and ignore it
7. Make Berwick-upon-Tweed Welsh, just for the hell of it
8. Throw in the towel – move to France

The Banderist Grows Old

Between 1943-45 a Ukrainian nationalist paramilitary group, informally named the Banderists, committed genocide in areas of Eastern Poland against the native Poles.

It is summer in his Lviv, and every year
he feels it more acutely through papery skin
as if his body is reducing under daylight.
His life is regular now, shrunken into a point.
He does not feel the need to wash his hands
before dinner, where he regularly eats
four potatoes, a carrot, a roll of bread. Watch, he
cuts the fish expertly, slitting it smoothly
from neck to navel. The knife is sharp, always.
There is no space between the borders of his days
for unnecessary movement, for questions, for debate.
Often, in his old age, he forgets his glasses
and if you asked him now where to dig
he doubts he would remember. His neighbours know
he is one of the heroes, last of the nation builders
in a country where everyone has seen blood
and no one asks the other whose it was.
He likes the sound of cats purring and afternoon traffic
just sitting and letting thoughts drift, back to a tree
a village, a courtyard
the well, sunshine
the rope
the axe
what happened there

The Gift

Often, after the tide had been good
and when my father had visited the homes
of those who could not afford to pay
I would lie awake into the dying evening
my eyes pressed tight shut, as if in prayer –
waiting for the gentle doctor's hand on my shoulder
before pretending to yawn and stretch from sleep
as he led me outside to the lemon tree by the gate.
They would be hung in plastic bags, shapes throwing
crazy silhouettes onto the lawn in a moonlit puppet show
or tied by tails on low branches – a surreal fruit
shells shining in rusted red, claws bumping softly together
like wind chimes in the soft Mediterranean night.
And only the waving poplars saw us, but promised not to tell
each time as we reeled in our catch, laying them carefully
onto the Renault 4CV's unsprung back seats
our fingers coarse from rough string and dry saltwater.
I'd watch as their antenna twitched and flicked with life.
No one on the island but us knew of their unnatural migration
back to the coast, slipping along moonlit roads until –
at last! – my father would haul them out onto the sand
and he would let me pick them up, one by one
hold them under the breakers long enough to wake up
and then slowly let them wriggle free, passing them back
to the ocean

Distance and Closeness: a tryptic

for Dick & Jenny

I. Tracing the ghosts of my grandparents up the Zambezi

Finally, after conversation had been found at the bottom of every dish and the inland tide of wine had risen to sufficient levels, my grandparents would lean back into themselves and talk of Rhodesia. They would speak of the time Grandad's police unit went to intercept poachers and instead found an orphaned lion cub out in the African bush, how it was adopted to eventually become the group's mascot and carried like a housecat for regimental photos; of large regimental dinners fuelled by bush meat and sherry that ended in drunken revelry, with my grandparents' chairs once being hidden so they had to pretend to sit for the rest of the evening to the general hilarity of the table; of my mother worming her way under the veranda's floorboards and being almost scared to death when she found a large rubber snake inexplicably nesting there; of raucous family meals in successive houses from Triangle to Zusape to Bulawayo; of generations of faithful dogs, Rhodesian Ridgebacks large enough for a small child to ride around the garden; of now-legendary safaris and picnics out in the bush, overlooking the Victoria

Falls as the water thundered down from one
in a tent encircled by a herd of elephants, and
between their bulks towards safety and the rising
adults would even retrieve the sacred shoeboxes
project slides up on the wall, lulling me to sleep
dulled Rhodesian blues and yellows slid past
Sometimes there would be the subtle pop
slowed to private introspection, broken
up through the decades as if from an
wouldn't be aware of any of this: I
end of the table, or sprawled on
breathing in the smell of dust
stealthily borrowed from his
carefully, unfolding with
great, lumbering, languid
continent, captivated by the
'unknown land'; imagining my
ferns and trekking over empty
over the pages eagerly, earnestly:
ritual, I never did manage to find

plain to another; of waking up
having to gingerly tread
sun. Sometimes the
from upstairs and
with their soft *clunk* as
the living-room furniture.
of another bottle as the talk
only by an image that bubbled
underground spring. But often, I
would be ensconced at the other
the floor with legs waving in the air,
and time from Grandad's old books
study; turning their pages slowly,
glee for the forty-sixth time the map of that
river as it rolled over the spine of the
surrounding blank whiteness labelled
intrepid grandparents pushing past jungle
mountains as I finger-traced its long line
but each time I completed this

their source

II. Inventory of the contents of my grandparents' suitcase on their journey from Bulawayo, Rhodesia to Heathrow, England

2 pairs of custom-made sheepskin jackets, double thickness to keep out the British chill

1 jumbled box of doll's house equipment – destined to be lost between endless floorboards

4 battered bush hats, dented by memories and missing their chin-straps

1 dog collar (without dog), kept simply as it could not not be kept

1 box of secrets, said to hold a human heart and sealed shut with wax

29 socks, one of which is still mourning its soulmate left on the floor of a cheap hotel room on a distant continent

1 signet ring belonging to Cecil Rhodes

3 small beads from the ruins of Great Zimbabwe, which hold the key to the purpose of the ancient site and which will be hunted for fruitlessly by archaeologists for decades to come

1 ceremonial sabre adorned with the BSAP crest, destined to be swung, stolen and fought over by generations of grandchildren

4 pots and pans, hopelessly trying to tessellate in the packed space

2 elephant tusks, reputedly given by King Leopold II of Belgium to his wife as a gift and bought in a flea-market in Nyasaland in 1954

1 wedding photo, framed (contains: 2 smiling faces, 1 old English church, 1 entwined future)

1 original document of the Unilateral Declaration of Independence – the heaviest item in this case

1 rubber snake, pulled unwillingly from under floorboards and dragged by the tail across the ocean

3 shoeboxes of photographic slides, each of these images containing more than this entire box

1 small, flightless stone bird, nesting in a pair of shoes – no one is quite sure what it is or how it got there

4 small African masks, kept almost ironically as souvenirs of a life they cannot attempt to summarise and which will hang in nondescript hallways in a succession of suburban houses

2 children, who are thinking of all the trees in the African bush left unclimbed and who have no knowledge of just how damp and cold their English winters will be

III. I visited you yesterday afternoon

and noticed the years that have passed
(how have all those years passed?)
and you have grown old together.
The front room, your projection hall
your Wunderkammer has gone
and Africa seems suddenly much further away.
Why is distance measured only in space?
You were in the garden, stating your existence
in flowerbeds. And you were in the study
(a different room, the same place)
painting yourself into your landscapes
over and over.

          You know
          I've never felt more like my grandfather
          than when I'm sharpening pencils –
          carving deep, finding the lead
          whittling an instrument soft enough
          to write in his voice

Acknowledgements

Enormous thanks to the wonderful team at The Poetry Business for making all of this happen, as well as to Ronnie & Dawn Goodyer of Indigo Dreams Publishing for their continuous and unwavering support.

Several poems here have previously appeared in Ben Ray's collection *What I heard on the Last Cassette Player in the World* (Indigo Dreams Publishing, 2019). 'The kindness of the eel' was published online in the literary journal *Algebra of Owls*, and 'Morning After' on *Milk + Beans*. 'The Discovery' was published in *Bath Magg*. 'The Gift' received third place in the 2019 Stafford Green Arts Festival competition and has been included in the anthology *For the Silent* (Indigo Dreams Publishing, 2019). 'The thoughts of Charles Byrne' was longlisted for the 2019 National Poetry Competition.